FIRE SHADOWS

FIRE SHADOWS

poems

Gwen Head

Louisiana State University Press   Baton Rouge
2001

Designer: Barbara Neely Bourgoyne
Typeface: Adobe Garamond
Printer and binder: Thomson-Shore, Inc.

ISBN 0-8071-2662-4 (cloth), 0-8071-2663-2 (paperback)

The author wishes to thank the editors of *American Poetry Review, Prairie Schooner, Southern Review,* and *Yale Review,* in which some of these poems have appeared previously. "Night Sweats" was reprinted in *The Pushcart Prize XVI: Best of the Small Presses.*

The author gratefully acknowledges the support of the Literature Program of the National Endowment for the Arts, grantor of a Creative Writing Fellowship in Poetry that made possible the completion of this book.

The paper in this book meets the guidelines for permanence and durability of the Committee on Production Guidelines for Book Longevity of the Council on Library Resources. ∞

for Katharine,
who taught me courage

CONTENTS

AUTHOR'S NOTE

In the fall of 1989, on the eve of her twenty-first birthday, my only daughter, who had been diagnosed some years earlier with bipolar disorder, voluntarily committed herself to McLean Hospital in Belmont, Massachusetts. She remained there more than a year. The poems, almost all in strict forms, that constitute the nucleus of *Fire Shadows* were written during that difficult and painful period.

"Mental illness" doesn't just happen. It is primed by genetics, molded by experience, assuaged by psychopharmacology, solaced by the love and concern of others. Among the young women who suffer most acutely from affective disorders, it is also culturally mediated—determined by an arbitrary expectation of the "normal" peculiar to a given place, time, class. Yet none of these circumstances, alone or in combination, explains the enormity of it—the terror, the valor, the mystery. By whatever name one calls it, whether the neutral, contemporary "mental illness," or the old-fashioned, histrionic "madness," it challenges, stretches, distorts, and uncomfortably expands our collective notions of what it means, not just to be "normal," but to be human.

Endeavoring to understand my daughter's ongoing ordeal, I found that I had first to reinterpret myself and my life. I reinvented my long-dead parents, Harry Gwen Head and Elsie Scott Head, and reimagined the marriage into which I myself had been born. And then I looked back on my own first marriage, at the man who was my daughter's father, at her childhood, and later, after the marriage ended in divorce, at our years as a mother-daughter dyad.

Besides these principal characters, certain outside observers and commentators also get their say. Those speakers whose identities may not be clear from context are named in parentheses, below the title of the poem and before its text. Dates, too, are important to certain titles. The most poignant voice of all belongs to my daughter Katharine. This voice, italicized throughout the rest of the book, is first heard midway through the "Kindling" section, in the poem "Bolivia." Thereafter the mother, who has herself grown up earlier in the book, also speaks out as "I"—although this "I," like Rimbaud's, is another.

Fire Shadows, therefore, can be read in several ways. While each poem stands on its own, each is also part of a sequence. These sequences in turn form a skeletal three-generation family novel. And I hope that both the individual poems and their arrangement contribute to the unifying metaphor of the book, which is the firing of the beautiful and austere unglazed stoneware of the Bizen region of Japan.

The late poet Richard Ronan, a cherished friend who died of AIDS early in the year of my daughter's hospitalization, left both his unpublished manuscripts and his Bizen teabowl to me. His example, these exemplars, have been constantly with me during the writing of this book.

ELDERLY PRIMIPARA, 1940

(ESH, in New Orleans)

Pot-bellied, owl-eyed, blurry-faced, jowly—

for this, my green sunrise in the icehouse,
bluebonnets, butter churns, nainsook corset covers,
Caesar, Josephus, rock and rye in hiding
behind a Bible freighted with genealogies.
In the pastoral distance, the stunned brown hulks of cattle
on our mesas, banquet tables heaped for slaughter.

For this, calla lilies, paired bergères,
and the chilly shine of calipers on green velvet.
Next, a much-traveled palimpsest of steamer trunks,
echoes, incense, pigeons—
Civilization!
And a bolt of Brussels lace steeped in desire,

to be folded away for a decade of held breath,
a decade of ring-bound alacrity, scurrying fishhooks,
until he, as prophesied, came:
eager, nervy, neat as a swain in shirt ad
with his rural kindness, his dazzled, bookish wooing,
his poverty.
                    Our poverty. What choice
had he, had I? A table is set and we eat.

For this the enema, the twilight sleep
the speeded-up, grating mechanics of extraction—
this mass of yowling protoplasm, size of a rump roast.
It has not my red hair,
yet is heir, if it lives, to much—

And I, elderly primipara, am both maker and donor.
Latinist father and judge, here is your posterity.
She, infant latifundist, Sunday's child!

CITY ROOM GLOSSY

(HGH and his fan club)

His daughter, who wants to grow up
to be Rube Goldberg, will live to love and puzzle
over this shot: a high-ceilinged room
filled with shadowy contraptions,
their connections and purposes unclear.

The largest construct has twenty biomorphic
components: eighteen upright,
uptight, hatted, and female;
one compound (male to decorous
female) and lap-seated, in the notch
of a large, scarred, horseshoe table,
under a second horseshoe
of metal pipe, from which hang,
shower-like, inverted cones
she will later, on faith, take for light,

since some parts—the time clock, the paste pots,
the pasha-like *déshabille,* Roi-Tan in hand,
of the slot man, reputed to look
like Clark Gable—seem perfectly clear.

But is housewifery or stenography
the second oldest profession?
For only in the comics
could these be girl reporters, since like Joe
Palooka or Alley Oop,
Brenda Starr is but one,

these, many:

receptionists, telephone
operators, even morgue
librarians. Whoever they are,

4

his wicked horn-rims,
his cocked black brows, seem to jeer,
Enough and to spare, little ladies.

And so they must take themselves
seriously, serviceably,
and (as the wife now lying
at home with a washrag over her throbbing eyes
might say) *keep rocking along,*
functional parts discreetly ornamented
—here a scarf, there a string of glass pearls—
and make what they can of the mystery
of their adoration, the infinitely long and versatile

assembly line that makes anything
and anyone, even Rube Goldberg.

SHOOTING STARS

(ESH)

Cracked eye to splintered
board, rusted standard, she
is lost in a gray nether firmament,
nebulous with spillage, spittle, stubbed-out brown comets,
its celestial music the carillon
of galvanized cans the late drunks crash into.

Up late enough to see as well as hear
these, she's really out here to search
the sky for her quick, cryptic sisters,
the child-maned, sky-wet Nereids.
For them we have made this steamy midnight picnic
on our balcony, at the shore
of the universe.

Harry in wartime
tan trunks, I in flowered bandeau
and shorts, a new white comber
of flesh at my waist, we are
naked, or almost, together.

We wait and we wait.
I wanted her to learn,
not just the sky, but patience.

A shower of meteors, I promised, a leaping seethe
of dolphins, an eye-squinting splash
of hurtling light. But these

come only once in a great while, each spark far
and smaller than a firefly.

Harder to find, it doesn't veer or wink,
but marks with platinum
calipers its little arc on the void,

and cuts it, coldly.
A degree, or two, or ten, of light she doesn't,
as often as not, see

—her head buried now in the figurative sand
of the quilt that smells of camphor, upchuck, mildew,
and of real sand, long ago,
real sweat, real lovemaking—

because how is she, or anyone, to know
when something, finally, is going
to happen? Or where? Or what
she was meant to learn?

CANAL STREET

(ESH)

They were called *aquarelles* when I still made them.
I don't anymore. And nobody now remembers
this street as water. What we call Canal
must once have been a quirk of the sluggish, mercurial
river, a wildness abruptly canceled,
then reclaimed with sandbags, pilings, tons of concrete,
to traffic again in spices, cotton, men.

Down the length of the filled-in thoroughfare, today
we ride a varnished clipper ship, its double
wake a track of shrieking iron. It scuds
between paired rows of self-regarding palm trees.
Its levees are plate glass storefronts bound with stone.
It's raining, and the city is redoubled
in slick, shifty light. I sit up front
with my unfinished replica, tired and whiny
from our thrifty walk up Bourbon to Canal.

But we've gone shopping.
The darkened world behind us
        —call it shadow, echo, or reflection;
            call it ourselves a dozen years ago—
hasn't and can't. It wears our broken straws,
split leathers, wilted daisies, funeral suits.
The clever watercolorist I used to be
might conjure such a murky nether world
not from paint, but a wash of dregs, lees, leavings.

Most doublings double back upon themselves,
it seems. Nothing is ever really
used up. I keep picturing
my fat sable brush awash in its fisheye mason jar,
slashed through pigment, then poised

thunderous, dripping, and splashed,
torrential, on white paper parched with waiting.

And after, that brush wrung dry, lusterless, jammed
in a chipped vase, with its fellows.

How often the mighty river has changed course,
I tell my daughter.
How it must, and will, again.

CINDERELLA

(ESH)

Transforming her into a drudge,
I dye for her art,
vat of tobacco brown on the gassy back burner,
my freckled arms mulatto to the elbows,
as I plunge and stir the tattered trousseau sheets:
frayed monograms, laddered hemstitch, nun's fine darnings
undone, the last
thin rags from my hope chest.

For my duckling is this year's princess designate,
she who was last year's jeering, cross-eyed Carabosse.
Ten scrawny years old, still jumpy
and preening, light to the hoist
of the burgeoning prince with strapped-down breasts.

Screened by the fat, gesticulating
fairy godmother, she must unzip
to ravishment—synthetic
chiffon and skewed, sequined tiara
hidden, all along, beneath rags.
As has been the box-toed racket,
the pink satin sheen below tatters,
that the audience will have somehow contrived
not to notice.

And I, while she triumphs?

Should the zipper jam, in the backstage dark, secreted
beside the cardboard carriage, awaiting its roll-on
part, I'll scrape the phonograph needle back
toward revelation, as many times as it takes.

For the leap to art demands both guile and clemency—
and these scores I know,
these grooves I have by heart.

SUMMER, APART

(HGH)

Some words I cannot write. Those that I do
begin *June, July, August*
—even *September* this year—
and end with my name,
just *Harry.*

    Dear Mrs. Head:

    The daily rain is falling
    so hard I can't get out, so will grab
    this moment to drop you a note.

    Annabelle is waging continuous
    war on the roaches with spray and poisoned potatoes.
    The best electric fan is on the fritz.
    More plaster fell in the kitchen. Mrs. Hamilton
    Polk Jones, traveling abroad, cannot be reached.

    The wage slaves on the almost solidly
    Guild copy desk at The Picayune *are howling*
    for restoration of the five-day work week,
    now that the War is over.

    Me, I take my ease on the rim.
    My incision's still not healed.
    I sprinkle sulfa on the raw spots twice
    a day, and leave the bandage off at night.

    How's the polio situation in Texas?
    I've sent Wrigley's to you and Gwendy,
    shirtboards that she can draw on, funny papers.
    I tried to deposit your Western Union check,
    but the bank demanded your signature.
    The rain seems lighter now. Let me hear from my gals.

Ruptured appendix, peritonitis, gangrene.
If not for those white crystals, I'd be dead,
not sleepless, lonely, sweating in the night.
Random houseflies light, tickle the hairs
of my oozing belly till morning.

Then I swig black overset
coffee, dress the wound in gauze, myself
in seersucker suit and snap-brimmed Panama,
leave Annabelle five dollars on the mantel,
and, out on the steamy street, post yet
another chatty, unassuageable letter.

Flame-haired kit fox, unfillable
void in my life, what has become
of man and maid, husband and wife,
father and mother?
                    Why
must I end each letter with my naked name,
but never the missing, the interdicted answer,
that long ago was
                    Love,

ALARM

(ESH, in transit)

The last time we moved
was wartime. She was so little
she flung herself sobbing under a silly, spindle-
legged table she loved, the right size for her to squat
in hiding, beneath the notice
of incomprehensible grownups.

A table that we had to leave behind.
I'd already called a taxi. The burly movers
waited with pallets and furniture wraps. I packed
one final box: pills, checkbook, unwashed dishes,
a Baby Ben alarm clock.
                              She howled on,
skirling and keening like a little fire truck.

Of course!
I palmed the siren song I'd found,
then, in the taxi, held it out to her,
wound its key, set its alarm to Now,
pinched her small fingers to its pin, then pulled.
"You're a brave Fire Chief, racing to rescue everybody!"

Winding, then pulling, she let the little clock
holler for her, down Saint Charles to Canal
to Bourbon, and hopped out glad at our new door.
Anything's bearable if you make enough
ruckus about it.

Or used to be. This time, it seems, there's no
ruckus left to make.
I'm fifty, going home—all three of us are—
to Mother for good: good schools, climate, doctors.
My daughter—she's that taciturn, hair-twisting
age—reads, only her eyes

moving, hours on end.
These silver streamliners
too, seem newly hushed—all but the gnashing
vestibules that link one car to the next.

No sound from the endless, dipping telephone lines,
no sound from my sullen daughter,
wound tight into her future.

Oh, it will all be so easy once we're settled—
nothing, any longer, to rescue
or be alarmed about—

now that my life's
run down.

ABUNDANCE, 1952

(ESH)

Because Mother worries about me, I go to the Garden Club.
She thinks I ought to go somewhere
besides the drugstore, the podiatrist,
Piggly Wiggly, the orthodontist, the bank,
the cemetery on holidays.
We save our Folger's cans to put the flowers
in—lilies at Easter, zinnias the Fourth,
chrysanthemums Thanksgiving,
poinsettias Christmas.

I drive us to the dead in Mother's brand-new
Roadmaster, air-conditioned, with chrome-rimmed air scoops
ventilating its hood.
"A four-holer," Harry calls it.
Vulgar, but then we both grew up on farms.
The difference is, I've traveled.

These leathery Texas flowers—well, they're not
the Luxembourg, or Whitman's lilacs.
That's how Harry won me: *Leaves of Grass,*
slipcased and numbered, with hand-painted boards
and deckled pages. Scrimped for and cherished.
Not like this year, when suddenly
there's so awfully much to buy,
all of it labor-saving, rich, unbeautiful.

Mother's the grower. I'm not. I just arrange.
My group did paired arrangements,
single color, no wires allowed.
I borrowed Mother's milk-glass horns of plenty,
two fat lavender snails slabbed like bookends.
Her showy cornucopias, though, looked scant,
strewing, rather than spilling, mostly chrysanthemums.
How was I to make them disgorge something lovely?

My Christmas check from Mother, the Southern Pacific,
suspense. . . . At last my shipment came, on time!

I came in third, but that wasn't the point.
Rather, the crate as big as a breakfront,
and our yardman borrowed from digging up the rose beds
for the umpteenth time, to tear it apart, with chisel
and crowbar, splintered board by splintered board.

Inside, tubbed in dry ice like homemade ice cream,
huddled a fallen star,
a boulder crushed to amethyst shards, the glitter
and pinch of cold upon them.

My lilacs!
Walt's. Poor Harry's.
Their scent like satin gloves stroking my body,
lemon ice, raspberries, Ponselle's Violetta.

And yes, half were withered—
frozen, drooping, bruised.
I smashed their stems, I nursed them with sugar water,
until their heart-shaped leaves began to beat,
and my broken doves rose up, and breathed, and soared
—a day, an hour, a moment, what did it matter?

I with them, knowing no more
than they what it all meant—
such difficult plenty,
ephemeral, never enough.

ALTERATIONS

(ESH)

I take my daughter to a bungalow
that smells of chalk dust. Behind its dim screened door,
a threadbare American Oriental, boards
beneath it scummed with decades of carnauba.
On the spindly what-not, a glaze-faced, legless belle,
porcupine-skirted with dress pins.
Beside her, shears, both plain and pinking, bias tape,
and a spinster's family album of pages razored
from *Vogue,* where the famished eye may safely graze.
Balenciaga by Horst. An hourglass
of silk gazar. Butterfly wings and famine.

I have brought my fledgling here for camouflage
for the scrawny chest, the hip skewed by the book bag.
The skirt must not cup, the gusset beneath the armpit,
newly shaved and freshly slicked with antiperspirant,
must yield but not bag.
They are both, we are all, so patient.
The younger must stand unmoving, as if hooked
upright at the apex of the long-closed fontanel.
The older, cactus-mouthed, must crawl in circles,
emitting locomotive toots of chalk,
while I supply the cultic chat of ladyhood:

> *Ou sont les soies d'autrefois?*
> *Ou sont les broderies d'antan?*

It should be some comfort that hems, at least, can be
set straight.
            But did I, even ever so long ago
when young and affianced, with intimate linens
minutely stitched (perhaps with secret prurience?)
by brides of Christ subsiding into blindness,

17

believe in any of this?
                      Must what we wear
become what tears us down in time,
most relentlessly when most beautiful?

ASPIRATION

(the family doctor)

Into the mound
of angry gristle
at the hinge of the girl's wrist, I stick the hollow,
embroidery-fine needle,
then lift the syringe's plunger.
The vacuum sucks the mushy synovium flat.

Skinny fingers steeled
to looseness, scarcely puckering
the sterile towel, she waits, stuck needle flapping,
while I fill a new syringe with Cortisone,
snap it on, ram it home, watch her wrist
plump with transitory healing.

For we have done this how many times already?
And today both wrists are bad.

A week from now,
pain-wracked again from practice,
she'll turn once more to steam, scalding basin,
patient kneading at bedtime.
                              The angels,
Bach, Mozart, Chopin, Beethoven, must shelter
her sleep. Her fantasy lover
could be that Polish chap the Tuesday Ladies'
Musical Club had to play here. Byron Somebody?

You are ruining your wrists, I warn her,
Forever.
            But I cannot make myself
say, *For nothing.*
Because if, in this sorry old world, there is such a thing
as ecstasy, truth

—call it what you will—
she has it,
she knows it.

I do it for the music,
she tells me. And,
It's impossible to do less.

THIRD YEAR LATIN, 1955

(Miss Hester Esson prophesies)

Crabwise, I scuttle up the ribbed stairs.
Heedless eddies of girls boil all about me,
effervescent, abrasive.
Not the crab but the wolf gnaws and mangles
my bone house. *Cartilago
delenda est,* I think, but never say,
faithful to Cicero, unlike my girls.

Giggling behind their Ovids, passing notes,
they parse and construe on the lam.
Today one even brazenly paints her fingernails.
Another, this semester alone, has worked
her way through Volumes IV, V, and VI
of *The New York Times Crossword Puzzles,*
edited by Margaret Petherbridge Farrar.

Passer, delicia meae puellae . . .

I try to read these sex-crazed twits Catullus,
but only the crossword puzzle girl looks dreamy.
When I drop the Latinate entrails of American
English into their girlish hands
—why *is* there not a parallel adjective, *puellile?*—
they mostly squirm, shriek, drop them.

All but the crossword puzzle girl, a cat
dismembering destined prey.
Perhaps she descries in heart, liver, lights
a life a bit like mine? Elect. Alone.

After class, I chastise my favorite miscreant.
"Pay attention *all* the time. You're going to be
some kind of writer."

Perhaps poetry?
If so, her puzzle-solving mind
may one day make a playful epitaph
upon my surname: Esson,
that's almost the Latin verb *sum,
esse, fui, futurus est.*
To be.

RECESSIONAL, 1958

(HGH)

After the weeks of inconclusive tests,
the barnstorming expert on carotid arteries,
the snoopy padres and sanctimonious deacons—

After they tied my old girl's wrists to the bedrails
and left her to croon the call letters, over and over,
of W-O-A-I, that used to broadcast
my singing commercials for Purina Chick Starter,
aired on the shit-kicker sunrise news at six,
the end—well, the end felt like a celebration.

My daughter slipped her mother's diamond rings
onto her own skinny finger.
Below, the plaza resonated
with the noise of crowbarred hubcaps, gonged and clanging,
and the mariachis sobbed in nectar voices,
serenading the whores at *Mi Tierra.*

My wife's mouth was open, in silent, sociable
chat with an out of season housefly, busy
and sterile as the mounds of ribboned flowers
we meant to cull to take home.
And Jesus dangled pensive, not well-dressed
either, chilly bronze in the air conditioning,
not even a sheet to tug up for privacy.

The night nurse hugged me. Then we almost danced.
Her gummy white shoes tangled with my wingtips.
Her straw hair and starched cap scratched my nose.
She cried real tears. Her cheap mascara dribbled
black down my collar. I knew the relatives
waiting at home would notice,
but say nothing.

After, we sat up for hours with fretful aunts
and cousins, drinking iced tea, talking plots,
obituaries, caskets—open or closed?
But all that while, the Gulf breeze kept on singing
its right, mighty recessional.
Gusts of honeysuckle
swelled and diminished, while a far tide turned.
The blind-slats swayed and crackled, then went slack.

After I thought they all had gone to bed,
alone in the butler's pantry, I poured and hoisted
a stiff one, in crystal.
"I'll just have a drink
with the little Elsie," I said out loud.
To myself, so I thought.

But out of the mahogany
and broadloom gloaming of the dining room
my daughter's voice responded.
"I don't think she ever recognized me
again, do you? Or knew who held her hand?"
She's barely eighteen.
I poured her one. We sipped
in silence.

A month ago, that only child came home
from school to find herself a stranger to
her frightened mother. I was at the bucket shop.
She called me there. The tape was running late
that bullish day. Braniff was going up
and up. And for that instant, we were rich.

KINDLING

INTERSECTION, 1963

America happens on wheels.
One young couple gets into a convertible,
with motorcycle outriders clamped
like remoras to its flanks;
another into a modest
Buick Special, a blue-plate lunch of a car.
What comes next could not happen in a world
more allusive, more illusory.

But America happens at right angles,
so, at the intersection of Commerce and Houston,
the Buick Special couple is forced to wait,
irked and hungry, at an unblinking
red light, its companion sign
blurting DO NOT CROSS,
while the limo couple sweeps by,

impromptu, she all new,
all pink, and radically redesigned,
he with a chrome-grilled grin for the non-occasion,
a windshield wave.

So close they could have leaned out and shaken hands.

Next night, the world-famous violinist
and friend to the famous, too shaken
to balance on the crags of the Bartok Concerto,
spills his guts, by way of the Bach
D minor Chaconne, out on stage.
That's harder to listen to, even, than the news
And truer.
            That day, the Buick Special couple,
its car thirsty, found out
at a filling station. Why
were so many gathered around

a broken-down Merc with all four doors wide open,
listening, as if it had just been invented,
to the radio?

And what could anyone do
after such knowledge, but fall in
with the listeners, the watchers, the ceremony?
Top-speed cortege to Parkland, grassy knoll,
stacked school books, sniper, vigil, flight, jail—
then lights, cameras, crowds, a hand with a gun,
the puny, implausible assassin, assassinated—

followed by all the stations (since America
happens in pictures) of the grainy, kinescoped wake
that ground on longer than Lincoln's funeral train,
at last co-opting (as people were starting to say)
its symbols: black horse, reversed boots—

yet leaving as intact as that "eternal
flame" at the tomb, the impossibility,
for both surviving young couple and grieving young widow
and children, of understanding how each came to be
where they were, and when,
and not to some other place.

DIORISSIMO

(a private duty nurse, Athens, 1964)

A twelve-hour shift
at thirty drachs an hour,
not bad, not good. It's cool
in the Blue Cross Clinic suite, shutters drawn
against the heat, both of them sulky,
having quarreled for hours before my day begins.
This was supposed to be their honeymoon.

But, *ponai,* she moans, *ponai.*
One third of her Greek. The rest is *kalimera,*
kalispera. She clenches both fists
to the ten-centimeter cut below the bikini line
slit and stitched by handsome Dr. Kouremenos,
trained in the States, and rich, almost, as his patients.

I set a Thermos of ice beside the fat
purple finger, streaked yellow, its stoppered
bottle like something behind the iconostasis
of a village church.
Tea, yogurt, orange juice,
toast, fresh figs. She doesn't
eat. He doesn't talk, except to read
the English paper out loud—another shepherd
struck by lightning. They've kept
a tally since her operation:
six in ten days. They seem
to find that funny.

Around noon, the back sitting room littered
with papers, his daybed unmade,
the stubbled, nail-bitten, child-
husband goes out. I'd guess
these two may be five years younger
than our spoiled boy king and his foreign bride.

She sits up to eat a bit,
then cries, paints her eyes, puts on
a fresh gown, cries again, sleeps

till four, when he comes back, uproarious,
reeking with ouzo, carrying a bow-tied box
of cream puffs, napoleons, éclairs,
bought at the bakery in the Athens Hilton,
where, I'm told, not just the baths
but the back stairs are marble.

I knit until her fever spikes. She's like
an eye-rolling pony then. I rub her down
with eau de toilette from the liter bottle
on the metal nightstand, crystal
with a satin ribbon, a checked and gilded label.

Another drunk apology, that perfume
called *Diorissimo.* Expensive, but it smells
like lily of the valley that's been gassed,
beaten, boiled, scorched, then soaked in alcohol.
I'd rather smell a goat than a rich woman,
but I put my arm around her waist and let
her lean on me to the balcony.

Still not a breath of air. But we hear a band,
then the building shakes—it's like a parade, a festival
to her, all day she waits for them to come—

the long iron snouts that ruffle the drooping leaves,
the tanks, the swaggering boys wearing rot and dung.

DEADLY NIGHTSHADE, 1970

(Husband)

My pages gather dust on the folding ping-pong table.
What do I know about wine?
It's just rotting grape juice, bottled
with fancy labels, what's left
of somebody's summer in Burgundy.
Not my obsession. I've been there just once,
don't speak the language, don't want to.

The tongue I speak to myself down here
in basement exile (where the ex-*au pair's*
gook boyfriend used to wake us up
at three each morning, sneaking out noisily)
is sci-fi, worlds where time's irrelevant,
where any kind of edge or pulse can kill.

Sci-fi and weapons: *Jane's* and *Knife Collector,*
Soldier of Fortune, Naval Review. My Japanese
swords bar the wall. Biplanes and bombers,
half-painted and coming unglued, crash in my closet,
among throwing stars, *nunchaku,* hand-forged hippie blades.
Not that peace works either.
Shelved above weapons are skis, rackets, cameras,
lenses never seen through.
So what if lasers are newer? If I broke
its bottle, Chateau Margaux would cut just as well.

This afternoon, the sudden quiet of
the freeway woke me up, its switch-lanes closed—
another singsong, shuffling demonstration
against the war. If I'd re-upped instead
of getting married, I'd be far away,
one of the marched-against, not the privileged
marchers, not that it matters. Both

are million-celled ant-minds tugging different directions,
equally stupid, choiceless, smug.

Today my wife's not marching. On the deck
beyond the chinked shades of my stealthy space probe,
I spy our baby daughter in her play pool,
splashing her mom, wee planet ringed with water.

Then there's a buzzing, grating
noise—not a mosquito,
but a siren, another.
Helicopters, tiny bullhorns.
I'm too far away to catch the meaty crunch
of nightsticks, the click of handcuffs.
But shadowy life forms stagger
and flail, between slats, through my binoculars.
As usual, *she* won't notice. But our Scottie
Jeremiah, his blameless eyes grieving,
the grizzled runnels of his pedigreed snout
awash, scents civil breakdown,
and howls, prophesying tear gas.
My wife scoops up the baby, swathes her head
in terry cloth, and flees.
Rocketlike, flares of spray ignite behind them.

Running, they trample lilies of the valley.
Its scarlet pips are poison. And the graceful
vine that dangles from the big-leaf maple,
brushing their fleeing heads—that's deadly nightshade!

She says I'm crazy, paranoid. But everything
could be listening, even the trees
trip-wired, ticking down . . .

FLUNKING KINDERGARTEN

(. . . and father)

Here in the land of the wee folk, we're enormous,
as are their wicked overlords, absolute monarchs
pretending to espouse democracy,
by wearing sneakers, jeans,
and sweatshirts liveried with their Ph.D.'s,
escutcheoned, Latinate, ivied.

They've espoused this school, "upward mobility,"
and Piaget, as, when I wed
my energetic wife, I espoused
sloth.
        When people ask
at parties, *What do you do?*
I reply, *As little as possible.*
But my wife won't let me out of being a daddy,
hence these gnome chairs,
for the least to-do yet.

We sit on gumdrop-colored baby ladder-backs
with raffia seats. Upon our conference table
three blocks, a loopy potholder, and *Pat
the Bunny,* our presumed
agenda. We squat, creak, parley
like grownups with other grownups
braced creakily as we, ironing boards
on which to steam, press, starch, hang up
one ruffled five-year-old.

> *She's ready to read. Why won't she? (Perhaps she's deaf?)*
> *She won't tie her shoelaces. (What's worse, she doesn't care.)*
> *She says she hates dodge ball. (Deficient upper body strength?)*
> *She nods off during math mat. (She* does *have a regular bedtime?)*
> *She complains the boys hog the carpentry bench. (We're totally*
> *nonsexist, committed to gender-blind achievement.)*

Gender-blind dunce, I'm stymied by the math mat,
too. Bad genes, no doubt. Should hopscotch add,
subtract, multiply, divide, do interest, amortize?

My wife bids Montessori, a grand slam.

Long after these kids have all grown up to be
hotshot getters and spenders, and our ungraded sprite
obliviously has pass-or-failed her way
into some life or other, I'll stay stumped.
For there's no other school will have *me*—

no, not even hard knocks.

COLLAGE, 1980

(a mother, single again)

Two boxes full.
                    But if you arrange the horrors
artistically, things still may come out right.
Not everything is ugly. Consider the stars,
gold, strict, quite crowded, trophies of your nine-year-old
musical prowess. And the finger cymbals, the shells
voluptuously beach-combed. But everything else is sharp,

and attests to, or hints at, violence. Only your sharp
eye can arrange the several sorts of horror
so they speak to each other, the grammar and syntax right,
yet unbalanced, toppling. The barbecue skewer, the stars,
the proof sheets that show you still glamorous, but old,
eyes glistering, liquid molluscs bulging from shells

of fatigue not far from decrepitude. Whereas the shells
of *his* lids, seen through a fisheye lens, look sharp
and follow you just as he does, everyday horror
you pretend not to notice. For Mommy must set to rights
Daddy's tarnished image, burnish the knife-edged star
of his bluff and swagger bid for their daughter, old

enough to imagine love for herself, same old
saw, same spike-heeled party, same classic shell
game the child has lost once already,
                                        when sharp
syringes lost their magic, leaving to horrors
of body and brain the young boy who ought, by rights,
to have grown up to love her. That each of us must star

in *some* sob story leaves untouched its power to startle,
its visceral plunge.
                    You stoop, pick out an old
tangle of gears and numerals, stripped of gold shell,

35

chain, fob. Dead-set Longines, two sharp,
the sleepless hour you're stuck in, minor horror
amongst the major. You rifle a box for its right

mate, a blunt chrome cosh, that once was the right-
bladed trochanter of a friend. Beside it, EKG stars,
the constellation *corda minor,* old
arrhythmic omen you hope to shake.
                                        Its shell
slapped shut on all, the copier, a Sharp,
cranks up and spits back out a smudgy horror-

show too camp to look right for a star
of your would-be magnitude, pained yet glowing, sharp-
pointed pearl born from a shell of old horror.

BOLIVIA

(and her daughter)

I hate the sea. I've always hated water
even as a baby, even in my bath,
or so my mama says. She likes it, herself.
She goes in the sea like a mermaid, and comes out
a monster, rubber fins slimy with eelgrass.
The beach boys watch her. They're supposed to watch
me, but I don't care, for I am queen
of an island state in the pool, where everything
is blue, like my bathing suit. It is called Bolivia.

Outside Bolivia, things are mostly brown
or green. Our little house by the lagoon
has green reeds by it, brown ducks swimming under—
a mother, her six chicks, like fuzzy bows
on a sleek kite tail. Mama duck wears blue
chevrons on striped brown shoulders. She is a spy
from my Bolivia. On the brown lava, wild
peacocks strut on petroglyphs.
It wears their tails to shreds. That makes them shriek,
tin whistles, from the tin that's mined in Bolivia.
But mama says they sound like humans quarreling.

I sleep on the Hide-a-Bed. But we each have
our own bathroom. My shower takes five minutes.
Hers takes an hour, the water must get cold.
I think that's when she cries.

Some nights a beach boy comes to the door
to say she has a phone call in the office.
Each time I have to tell him she can't come.
That hateful noise of water crashing down—
I play with my hair until he goes away.

Tonight was luau night. We got dressed up.
Mama bought me a muu-muu, blue hibiscus,
ugly, but she meant well. The little orchid
on my plate was smeared with pork fat. After dinner
the beach boys put on skirts and leis and danced
and played the ukulele. So did the maids,

and then we had to pack. We bought Bolivia
here, so there wasn't room in any bag
to take my island home.
We tried and tried to make the air bleed out,
we even jumped on poor Bolivia,
but couldn't make it fit. "A four-buck air mattress,
I'll buy you another." I wanted to shriek and fly
at mother. But I just said, "There isn't any
other," and shrugged and turned my blue back on her.

Tomorrow morning we have to get up early
to fly back—where?
Having the same address is not the same
as home. I know Bolivia wasn't a real country
but pretend I don't. There are better things than real.

Bolivia was just blue plastic and air
with a leaky valve. It smelled awful, like chlorine.
But it sparkled, it stayed afloat. It was all mine.

SPACE CADET

There must be life out there,
incredibly, immeasurably far.
Or else why must I wear antennas
pronged from temples to mouth,
lashed tight with rubber,
all the time, but especially
—there's less static then—
while I sleep?

Beneath the velvet headband
that's supposed to make torture pretty,
there's stainless steel.
Mom could plug me in and fry me.
But it's you, distant double,
I need to hear calling to me
in your language of pings, squawks, thrummings
from the heart of the vortical, binary
star that bore us both.

There are four each week in my row
on the spaceship Orthodontia.
We lie on astronaut couches,
of plastic, synthetic grape-colored.
A mechanic tightens our screws, tests our bands,
all A-Okay. But the others aren't true voyagers.
They've bought the cover story: pretty mouth,
straight smile, shiny teeth.
                                    The better
to eat *me* with. Yuck, yuck, *says the Wolf.*

I don't ever want a boyfriend. Space is better,
black void I can shut my eyes and tumble into
anytime. Though lately,
eyes open, I see both earth

and limitless nebulae, all at the same
time, in the same space.

It's then, whatever then *means, that my Mom*
comes and taps on my forehead, asks, Anybody home?

DISORDER AND EARLY SORROW

Help me, Dr. Joyce Brothers.
                          What would *you* do
with one kid, twenty, male, outdoors lamenting,
worst among many woes, his dilatory
and probably irremediable virginity?

And indoors, another, female, fifteen, dead
still for two hours behind a locked bathroom door—
not a whimper, retch, or flush?

Outdoors, the vagabond son of an old friend,
is not really outdoors. His habitat is a hermitage
on wheels, a much-recycled
Volkswagen camper craggy with spare batteries,
fuses, Pennzoil, Pop Tarts,
its ornamental foliage four weeks' worth
of unwashed laundry.
His *Wanderjahr* is gilt-edged, his depression
soothed by a single plastic, multipurpose
tool. Issued by AmEx to his trust,
it's less confusing than a forty-two
piece wrench set,
or a woman.

Indoors, again entreated, soundlessly
slides dead bolt back, and manifests herself
hunched, mussy, tear-slimed, shuddering
between the bathtub's claws.
                          She's downed
the shower-curtain rod, spewed hoarded ribbons,
earrings, barrettes, eyeliner, hosed the whole
mess down with shampoo and peroxide—
even the fallen shower curtain, knotted
with pantyhose, even the tattered
copies of *Vogue*.

What *I* could do, Dr. Joyce, wasn't much. Outdoors,
ravenous with grief, requested a ham
sandwich. No, make that two,
with lettuce, tomato, mayo.
Indoors preferred to order off the menu:
soap opera, madhouse, pills.

THE TREMBLING

What we can't tell each other speaks through your body.
Limb wars with limb. You tremble everywhere.
The symptoms, the prognosis point to God,

who may be like you: bruised, amorphous, sad,
stirring in spasms, foundering on a stare.
What we can't tell Him, too, speaks through your body.

I am your duenna, you my pretty lady.
My firm hands draw a ribbon round your hair.
Your symptoms, your prognosis? Point to God,

who can tell drugs from madness, good from bad.
The worthy doctors murmur of a cure.
What they can't tell is speaking through your body.

I ache to be your high-jinks laughing bawd,
to show what waits to love you everywhere.
Your symptoms, your prognosis point to God,

as mine do. As all do. Trembling, we laud
an oceanic nostrum called Despair.
What none can tell another speaks through your body,
its symptoms, its prognosis. Point to God.

EXHORTATION

I warn my students against "the hortatory
you," its strangler's paws, dragging them into
poems, lives, not of their making, not
of their living, places they never wanted to be.
As I don't, in your poem now tending toward the epic
(though ripped, poisoned, exploded, flattened—then
pasted, in the postmodern style, to the cringing

page), want to be when words start to detonate: *bingeing,*
purging, bulimia, tactophobia, spend-
ing disorder, schizo-affective, masochistic—
such megatons of woe, all MIRV'ed at me.
The small words died. I liked *will* best. Or *grace.* But,
I can't help it, you say.
                              I say you have to begin to
help it. And *me.* Speak plain. Not cant. Nor oratory.

LAVENDER

Meanwhile, the humblest things keep trying to heal us.
The lavender has shriveled, flower to pod.
How did you learn so much about gardening? you ask,
idler, know-nothing *fainéante* by choice.

THIS-IS-YOUR-MOTHER-SPEAKING! Tape my voice
to idle with you, lonely. Dearest, I won't fuss
or do more than take you to this smallest task:
snip the square stems with shears. Buddha or God

smiles behind stenciled celadon, fat seeds
wrapped in peekaboo vegetable tissue, prestigious
as a box-shaped Japanese melon, bow-tied, provender
too fine for gullet or mind.   Am I getting religious?

But no one can die, can think or do bad deeds
whose hands are pungent with lavender.

THE BABY DREAMS

Sponge plastic with chromium nipples,
in an aspic of K-Y jelly,
set down on my chest in a ragged pentagram—
I awoke with the supernumerary
tits I should have had
as witch, as she-wolf mother
of ravening nations.

But, *Principessa,* you
are my sole rebellious protectorate,
and I thought the dreams would end there,
once the surgeon had gathered and tied
the fanned sheaf of my fertility,
each tube a knotted fetish, grainy head
still ripening one kernel at a time.

When did one first come to haunt me,
ghost of the future, launched toylike
down the greased ways of my spine,
sharp cookie-cutter mouth piercing the thin
yeasty skin of my chest?
Could I take it to school in my bookbag,
crook it on an arm playing soccer,
while I bled and bled into my gym shorts?
When I asked, its counter-weighted
eyes thudded sullenly shut.

Its siblings accumulated.
At twenty, at thirty, at forty,
I woke up in bed with strange babies:
robust babies that shouldered me out of bed,
ectoplasmic infants made from won-ton dough,
flower babies with limp, snapped necks
whose heads I was doomed to hold up forever.

This morning a red baby
slid out of a stovepipe under a tweed skirt
like a trick hand from a magician's sleeve.
Like life, the babies are bloodier now
and have read the books I read.
This one was a hunk of liver with raisin
eyes and a villainous voice.
It begged to go everywhere with me.
It left butcher paper smears on my cashmere twin set.

And here you are, neither bloodless nor bleeding,
but the milk and rose colors of life,
around your neck, a miragelike
archipelago of pearls,
your willed golden hair
drawn back, segmented
by barrettes and burnt-out roots,
into a map of warring states,
much like the murderous internecine strife
that rages in the brain beneath.

I know these uncivil wars.
The same thing still goes on
in my belly. Each thwarted red pearl
of the strand of generation and generations
is a tyrant, suffocating,
a potentate raging, like you, for breath and territory.

But only one may live. The rest I bequeath
to you, as dolls for your play, only daughter.

FIRING

HARVARD YARD, FALL, 1986

Vases of sky-borne earth, arranging blue-
fringed light into cutwork, what have they to do with you,
erl-child, pensive at your new, old window,
wearing the new name I talked the bank into
believing in, as you, still raw
from the moult of the old, could not?

All day long we have borne each other—
computer, duffels, crazy quilt, the shaggy
stuffed Himalayan cat you planted, standard
that made of your slack, cornered cot a motherland;
borne, too, the harryings of institutional jollity—
the Glee Club hell-bent on warbled self-deprecation,
the picnic, belated, scant, that brought to ground
good tweeds and scuffless shoes on the venous grass
and mitered copings of rosy, vestigial Radcliffe.

Now we peer through two dozen waning eyes. Below,
they are still at it, big children who seem to have known
each other forever—insistently heterozygous,
polyglot, demotic—all kinds of people, a few
of buildings, but just one dappled light
imbued with all the wistfulness of reason:
light of New England monoculture, erotic
cult of the doomed, gilded elm.

Not your native light, not my own.
Sanguine, stippled, raw, ours glares back from your future:
its airy seethe, its cutting, breathless flame.

FOUR POEMS

(for Richard, in San Francisco)

i. Night Sweats

"Bit by bit, grain by grain, the self is taken away.
The other men in my room were covered with KS:
gray skin, tubes everywhere. But they're in a conspiracy
with the doctors, and keep on hoping.

"The night sweats are terrible.
Liters of water—I feel myself dissolving.
But in dreams my body is real, intractable.
In one, I had huge stone hands, red thread, a needle—
the eye impossible to find. I woke up crying.

"In all my dreams, there is—call it a *feeling tone.*
During one of these stomach things I was convinced
I was pregnant, the baby was ramming and kicking me.
All that night two things were physically evident:
One was that there were two of me, the one on the left
bigger, the one on the right, smaller.

"And the other—every time I woke up
and realized I was lying in a pool of sweat,
I knew that this sweat was a woman,
a female that had come out of my body.
And I kept saying to myself, 'It's not you
that's sick, Richard. It's this poor
woman, this palpable female entity.'

"At one point, a couple of nurses came in.
I was drugged, convinced I was delivering
a child, and that it was *their* child.
Over and over I dreamed this, a hundred times . . .
the birth of my child, whose face I never saw."

ii. Submission

"They like a pretty eroticism, neat and lyrical.
Still, they've always rejected me with that eager
respect that invites recidivism. I confess
I know this work's too violent for them, too tough.
This poem was the last I wrote before Bill died.

"With, through, beyond him—I, too, had begun
some oceanic process. There was a setting sun
at the beach at noon that day. It's all mixed up with water,
his wish to be buried in water, what I tried
to write, not knowing where a deeply sexual
love *goes,* that major shift to becoming bodiless.

"I didn't get enough.
I didn't get enough.

"If I come back, it must be as a tiger."

iii. Home Care

"The first night was dykes on bikes,
this awful woman, my alleged night nurse,
who showed up in a state of psychotic rage and roamed
the apartment, sobbing, smashing her fists against
the wall, finally falling, as if pole-axed, asleep.
Then, innumerable sick—people with flu, coughs, fevers.
One woman arrived, her uniform flecked with vomit—
she had just thrown up in her car.

"Half don't speak or understand the simplest English.
Two different people, the first week, nearly burned
the place down—choking clouds of black smoke billowing
from the kitchen, as they read or knitted unconcerned—
they had tried to run the dishwasher without water.
Once the dispatcher had no one to send but her son.

A little thick, so another fellow came along
to 'help.' Enormous men—
                              Gwen, they were like big dogs,
mastiffs lolling in the hall outside my room.
I had to climb over them to get to the bathroom.
The friend—I had thought he was straight—got bored,
went out, and hit every bar in the Castro. At five,
he collapsed in sleep on my fragile antique sofa.

"I suppose they're decent people. I suppose they mean well.
But there's no privacy—they rummage through my papers,
they take things down from the wall and peer at them.
No, nothing's been stolen, no one has hurt me yet.
But how, *how* am I ever to get better
with all these marauding strangers in my house,
so like the disease that savages my body?"

iv. Ladies of the Farthest Province

Holding my hand, dozing, he says he dreams
of dying in the sheltered garden of my house.
His wrist is narrower, his hand finer, than mine.
In his garden, creeping mint has blackened under sun,
duckweed overgrown the carp pond,
climbing its rock verges in green shirring and ruches
spangled with watery rhinestones
like the faded denim jacket—once his father's—
each friend has worn and coveted.
Are the carp still alive?
Only one red sliver undulates through the black
and burning water shadows.

On his birthday he gives clothes away.
To one the black and indigo striped sweater he wore to the hospital.
To me a wondrous kimono
where flame-colored *koi* loll in braided, tiger-striped shallows.
I have no obi, no sash,

only my wide shoulders, my mannish *gaijin* stride.
He gives us all the grace of his imagining.
Anne-Marie, Maz, Terri, me—
                              "Oh, my faithful ladies,"
he murmurs, a novice swimmer still,
slipping through freshening currents of Xanax and morphine,
as he practices falling asleep.

Which of us has seen a carp in a wheel of ice,
flamingos feeding on the red of berries and ironstones?
Harried and graceless, we are women of the city, the moment,
sworn to be with him at the end.

BARBIES

Rediscovered in the attic, your old cut-ups,
hair hacked and dyed with ink or watercolors.
From wrists and ankles, granny knots of bondage dangle.
Some, like your hallucinations, are blithely shorn of limbs
and strut on only one of those improbable long stems
all all-American girls need, the better to mangle,
the better to twist and pop in painless dolor.
Be like me, they whisper. No way to make them shut up,

so now you'd like a newer foundling, store-bought,
with clothes, furs, jewelry, real estate, and pelf.
A bride, yes, but with a career of daunting authority—
president, maybe, of Mattel?
                    I pray, instead of yourself,
you slash, as you used to, the witless plastic naught
you sue for on the eve of your majority.

THE ARM

As the doctors tell it, things are always splitting.
Your mind's a permeable shale, you slipping through

    like iridescent oil. When the fit comes,
    your "irritable focus" kicks off bits
    that must be memory: worst was a man
    out walking his severed arm. A foot from the shoulder,
    it bobbed and dawdled, a gag leash without a dog.

    Yes, I was scared, but knew it wasn't real.
    There was no blood, and so I walked between—
    Pretty as any college girl, well dressed,
    in your too-long coat from Saks Fifth Avenue,
    its hem double-lined against the Cambridge mud.

But where and how and if *was he? And now?*
Is he, is it, *as lonely as I am?*

ON BEING BLONDE

I don't want to be blonde any more.
It's been fun, but it's like I have Dynel
hair. A hundred a month's a big bite.
And I can't even wear it down,
since my face is so round.
My hair's like a colander. Basically, it's a shell
to stuff with fillers and proteins, or to highlight
while it grows out. It makes me feel like a whore,

because everything else—even my shrink—can wait
but my hair won't wait.
                    And that's rough. I've had three psychotic
episodes so far this term. In one I mutilated
myself again, both arms. But no scars. Antibiotics
and vitamin E work great, though I did lose a lot of blood.

He doesn't love me. He said no one ever could.

THE MARINES RAISE THE FLAG
AT IWO JIMA

(the mother's psychiatrist)

She says she's fed up with talk, transcontinental
phone bills outrageous, blood pressure up. Not now,
then, ever, *did* it do, *will* it do any good.

Hence, wisecracks: extra miles, odometer
rolled countlessly back. Then there's
the one—you're in it Doctor—in which
the Marines monumentally land at Iwo Jima.

As she talks, I picture rucked-up bronze.
Before that came the photo's heaving grain,
the doughy, rain-slick mud:
    rain that glued fatigues to haunch and bicep,
    rain that poured highlights on helmets, cheekbones, chins,
    rain strung out in taut diagonals
from the tense haft of the manic, starry flag.

Years, dollars, doctors, tears, to what end?

She makes *me* the end Marine, reaching for meaning
as she strains to stub her daughter into claiming
something an indifferent world
might see as conquest.

But what if her child's banner was meant to be
fluid and wayward, its weaving to fray, its seams
to open in dangerous bloom?

We know now that photo was faked.

In the glamorous mire of metaphor, maybe not
the girl, but this still youngish woman,

knotting Kleenex, stands for the shreds
and thrashings, the vincible banner of reason aloft

in the mire, the torrential wind
of a daughter's madness?

WRITING THE THEME ABOUT *TESS*

There was a circle of people, playing a game like dodge ball
or keep-away or red rover. The ground felt like glass.
I kept trying and trying to reach, afraid I'd fall.

There was every kind and color of whizzing ball,
and every kind of pitch, dribble, or pass
around and across the circle playing dodge ball.

I had to guess at the rules. No umpire's call,
no whistle stopped the throwing, at or past
me, trying to reach, afraid to fall.

Then I noticed a colored letter on each ball.
And I realized the circle was my class,
the competitive circle of people playing dodge ball.

And somehow I had to catch every single ball
with the letters I needed to write my theme about Tess.
I kept slipping, lurching to reach, afraid I'd fall.

Red, yellow, commas, quotes—I snatched them all,
one by one, from the hostile air. But the fear was no less,
next day in the circle, playing the game like dodge ball,
running and lunging for thoughts, afraid to fall.

LEAVING

Two hours to read twenty pages. No, not that hard,
it was Milton. But next morning I woke up feeling terrified.
I went to the vault, to Bay Bank, and sat with my grandmother's
jewels awhile. That helps to calm me sometimes.
It wasn't enough that day. I went out, I made myself
go to my class on The Portrait. *I can't concentrate*
on anything spoken either.
                              You've got to understand,
I have what my father had, I am what he is,
and there is something missing in both of us—
the ability to be a working force in the world.
So, after two sentences I got up, I had to,
and left. Forever.
                   Now suddenly it is Always,
and I want only to live in myself, my damaged brain,
leaving no mark of my presence on the earth.

BLUE ON FIVE

So I wasn't with Richard.
I was a continent away
staying at an emporium of sorrows
from which shuttles ran regularly
to the palace, museum, and gardens
of madness.
But I preferred the taxi drivers, who were kind,
and had been there themselves, or knew someone who had.

Each floor was a different color.
Mine was orphanage blue.
A tunneling color, committed to cover-ups,
it skulked, usurping light.
What scraps and chinks remained
rode the chambermaid's cart, a chariot electric
with blanched towels and glistering ranks of spray cans.

Smeared mirror, bursting waste can
of grief, I blundered out and into
it, and into her arms.
                         Richard, you were two
interminable days dying.
For the better part of a blue,
blue hour, she held and rocked me, a clumsy stranger,
oozing and bundled, shipwrecked between dead friend
and mad child.
                    Of course her crooning couldn't
change that, or anything.
On green four, honeymoons foundered in dejection.
Jaundiced families quarreled on mustard three,
and if anyone still cared, both professional
and amateur lust, in russet,
held convenient sway on two.

Forty-eight hours.
Back rubs and jokes.
Morphine.
Drowsing, I think you dreamed
and sent a scouring angel of the azimuth
with feather-duster wings, to point my eyes,
like yours, safely toward home.

BALLADE: SELF AND NOT-SELF

These things start early. Each time you came in
to your own room after absence, you would seek
out favorite books, toys, animals; first check
each idiosyncrasy of fur, wheel, spine;
then gather and marshall them all. A stout front line
might not hold fast. No, each must be one spoke
in a stilled circumference that would not break
whatever the steep velocity of time.
These are my things, the things that make me mine.

Christmas, fifteen years later. Welcomed back,
you practiced aversion, shut doors and lowered blinds.
Regurgitated grass, fur, bone bits, rug twine—
the hall was your hairball. Bilious, you brooked
no taste of others, but upchucked my alarm clock,
your father's sock, an old friend's Valentine
like a prissy old cat—you whom I thought my kitten!—
to feast on dead dolls, eyes blank, limbs stained, manes hacked.
These are my things, the things that make me mine.

Where you've sent yourself now, the staff had never seen
or toted so much identity. Swiftly locked
down, you relaxed.
                    Next day I scrabbled through sea wrack
in your fetid basement: spavined slingbacks, magazines,
dirty clothes, journals, music boxes, knick knacks,
mirrors, earrings, sewing kits unraveling . . .
And shopping-bagged stashes of lithium, Depakote, Navane.
And your baby powder spilled, dispersed like smoke.

These were my things, the things that made me mine.

MATRON

It's another campus, she says. And it is:
a campus with newer brick, dejected trees,
and, marble and mauve with fountains, a toney eatery
named for a dead director. The security
is vastly better, also. In quintuplicate,
I fill out a requisition to see my daughter.

At her age, I was an inmate of Virginia
Hall—don't laugh—a freshman women's dorm
at Southern Methodist University.
There, boyfriends had to sign us out like books
with uncut leaves or dog-eared, on reserve
in either case, lent until midnight, weekends
only. So is she on reserve for life,

or has my card expired? Whence come the chintz
slipcovers, spool-railed stairs, albino ivy,
—such stalagmitic, blanched, infernal decor—
all institutions share, *in loco parentis?*
And is the blue-rinsed Matron here ensconced
a literal troglodyte, imperial
concierge of all these grottoes of the mad?
She rips her copy off, hands the rest back.
My chilled and dozing cabbie starts awake
and skids up the black-iced hill to Codman I.

What Georgian stoop is raw concrete, what vestibule
linoleum and wire-glass? Where is Diana,
poised on one toe, with bow and incandescent
globe? Instead, I feed the Coke machine,
buzz, and deal from the top my flimsy, carboned
permit to mother. And then I track you down,
shelved, in the lounge, the one inmate not smoking,

my virgin huntress stalking skittish quarry,
my book of rare hours under lock and key.

SOMNIA

Less and less stately, in chambered disarray,
your soul shrinks to sleep. Your chevroned quilt's at war
with the zebra light of noon behind closed blinds.
For twenty years I've known that swag of hair,
those eyelashes, that hand of glazed white porcelain.
As a small child I coveted such a hand,
forget-me-nots and ribbons in its palm,

where grown-up ladies stubbed their lipsticked butts.
Your shuddering's almost stopped. Marine, becalmed,
you drift on a Sargasso Sea of Navane.
Your bad dreams stay. Life's horrors, left behind,
make nightmare sweeter than the light of day.
No one can see the knives, the blood, the rats.
No one but me can guess your laddered scars.

ZEBRA

You can't be like me because you don't like me.
Either me. The one who's immoderately smart,
pretty, beloved, a little famous even.
Or the one who's frustrated, dim, has failed her art,
and ruthlessly lives her thwarted life through you.
There are two *yous*, as well, to tease apart,
two versions of each almost-death, each friend
turned foe, each poisoned cure. Twos take their toll,
a drawbridge lifted anywhere you start,

that shrieks and sticks, two striped *V*s in the air.
You can't and can't get over anything.
Sometimes you try to change. You've let your hair
begin to grow in dark, a spreading smoke ring.
Zebra, you call yourself. Pitch striped on glare,
clashing at angles, a splayed skin on the floor.

ART THERAPY

Remembered, the mother is dismembered,
a woman of flat, painted parts that yearn to be sculptural:
Her pediment of black and white Ionic curls,
her green, island eye, its tides of wine-dark, shameless
eyeshadow.
       Fearsome the slit between lips,
the clawed scrawl of red at each cheek,
the crow's-foot arrow trephining the ringleted temple.

Whereas the child artist's face is *all* winsome as a dimple,
swept clean by a flaxen broom of perfect blamelessness.
Her eyes are a kittenish turquoise. But no! For, stripped
of the mawkish, the mock, those eyes are diamond embers
vised in blue steel. And the rosebud mouth is visceral
as a hate-pinched anus. Yet, from the mother's breast, a seek-
ing spurt of foliage twines,
                by which the child is made beautiful.

LIQUID PAPER

Jeff is the sweetest man she's ever met.
Jeff has no privs. He sends her out to buy
what? Liquid Paper. So, what does he need *that* for?
"Art therapy."
                  Thin studio white won't bury
bright colors deep enough. He wants a blizzard
in April, in August. "Any month is great for snow."

Six bottles, and already he needs more.
"Come on, what is it really for?"
                                "I'm making
a bomb," he says, deadpan.
That scares her. She thinks he really could, and would.

He is the most powerful man she's ever met.
Made bigger bucks than his dad, some pompous muckety-
muck party hack, last year. He'll turn nineteen
ten days from now. Then she won't feel so old.
"It won't kill anyone, won't hurt, just make a mess.
White flakes all over. We know the joint has dandruff
already. What's the big fucking deal?"

He is the funniest man she's ever met.
Between baggy sweater and blousy camisole,
five bottles ride back. But then he needs eight more.
She asks. He snaps, "I'm plastering up the hole
in my nose. Just get them, okay?"

She does. He keeps the stash. His roomie rats.
And the loony bin narcs shake them down and out and up.
Clothes on the floors. Drawers emptied on the beds.
Hers. Jeff's. The Kid's. The Rat's. It's two A.M.,
they're crying, huddled in the hall, her ruffled nightdress,
their grungy briefs.
                        No, how could *she* have known?

she wails, grinding her grandmother's gold filigree
bracelets from Tiffany's over the fretted blue
and pink at her wrists, nice girl that she is.
                                    He's putting
his fists through the mullioned panes of authority. Watch
the glass bleed, the wood bones snap! *That* won't white out.

She called him the gentlest man she'd ever known.
So now it's his time to wrench out the telephone,
mute money-changer, and hurl it from its crude
plywood temple.
                    One month already. She says
she's never loved anyone else like this. She even
says they're engaged. That must mean something, she's smart.

He'll have three days in the quiet room to cry,
daydream, jack off.
                    She's never let him touch her.

PANTOUM OF THE SUICIDES

It's getting dark now. Let's tell stories about suicide.
There's nothing on the tube, not even Star Trek.
The ones who do it best, of course, are gone.
But we do it well, or else we wouldn't be here.

There's nothing on the tube, not even Star Trek.
Mine is the usual story: sharps and pills.
I do it well, or else I wouldn't be here.
You must know lots of stories. Don't be shy.

Even the usual story, sharps and pills,
takes cunning, skill. You plot to get the stuff.
You must know stories, too, guys. Don't be shy.
No matter how you do it, it takes guts,

cunning, and skill to find and stash the stuff,
to get the dose right, wait for the right time.
Or hide, then slash! Yes, doing that takes guts!
But when everyone's your enemy, any tool will do,

any dose is right, and any time the right time.
Did you hear about the kid who slashed his wrists with a toothbrush?
If everyone's your enemy, any tool will do.
Don't laugh. He was as serious as you or me

—that boy who slashed and slashed at his wrists with a toothbrush—
as serious as the lady who took a hundred Nembutals.
He wasn't laughing. He was as serious as you or me.
Three docs called the woman brain-dead. But she lived,

dead serious, that lady who took the one hundred Nembutals.
One doc wasn't sure, so nobody pulled her plug.
The docs called the woman brain-dead, but she lived.
That's wild, but not the wildest story I've heard.

One unsure doc, and nobody pulls the plug.
Another woman, divorced, a shrink with a kid
—listen, this one is wild, the wildest story I've heard—
and she found out she was bipolar! She wanted to die,

that woman, divorced—that bipolar shrink with a kid!
She bought lots of insurance. Her son was maybe ten,
and couldn't know bipolar Mommy wanted to die.
So she had to keep it from looking like suicide.

She bought all that insurance to bring up her son, aged ten.
So what happened next? She sliced a tomato open.
She had to keep it from looking like suicide,
so she mixed the tomato pulp with yogurt and blood.

She took the tomato, like this, and cut it open
like you'd cut a wrist, only that was too crude for her.
She mixed the tomato pulp with her own blood,
and let the mess steep at room temperature for a week.

To cut her wrists would have been too crude for her.
But she had the guts to shoot that stuff into her veins,
that mess she'd steeped at room temperature a week.
Bacteria, molds with an appetite for her blood cells—

she had the guts to shoot them into her veins
—infections already primed to overwhelm her,
bacteria, molds that fed on her white blood cells—
through a tiny needle, a tiny vein in her hairline.

The infection was already primed to overwhelm her
with fever, delirium, solitary death.
Tiny needle flushed away, tiny scab at the hairline.
She was steeled for pain, convulsions. But not the vomiting.

Fever, delirium, solitary death,
all for her son. But a neighbor heard her retching,

saw the horror of her convulsions and her vomiting,
and called an ambulance to take her away.

All that for her son. If the neighbor hadn't heard her retching,
she would have died. No one ever would have known.
But the ambulance came screaming to take her away,
and make her another story of failed suicide.

Maybe she still wanted death, wanted no one to know?
But it wasn't her choice. Not dead. Not alive. In a coma.
It's way too dark for more stories about suicide.
The ones who do it best, of course, are gone.

FIRE SHADOWS

TRIPLE SESTINA: HER DREAM

I am a passenger on a train that must be the Orient Express.
Firebox stoked cherry red, it explodes
through the dusk. Within, all is rosewood, crystal—self-
indulgence as art form. Outside, the whistle dies,
keening like a swan strangled by swirling snow,
yet unheard by the cosseted passengers, safe from all danger.

But still there is a lurking sense of danger,
a mortal fear too subtle to express.
And yes! There is *a presence that explodes*
behind me, sinks its claws deep in my self,
and wrings, pins, throttles to make me die,
strangling me till my failing sight's like snow.

Yet the passengers sip, read, nap, ignore the snow,
a blizzard now, outside. Somehow my danger,
my struggle, bores or repels them. Inexpress-
ible ennui's their style. So, sheer rage makes me explode,
burst from the strangler's grip, propel myself
with the force of death itself, away from dying,

yet deeper into nightmare.
                        For, facing me, with dyed
blonde hair, black brows, blue eyes, and skin like snow
—each grace, each idiosyncrasy—I see the dangerous
smile of my double: *My Self, whose friendly expression*
of greeting drips nitroglycerin, set to explode.
Literally. Says My Self, "You needn't think *your*self

"safe. You broke my grip. But I, My Self,
have limitless weapons and ruses to make you die.
Somewhere (perhaps it's buried in the snow,
tuned to vibrations; as the train passes, danger
and death! Or tucked in a cranny of the sleek *Express,*
any one of its forty cars!) a bomb waits to explode!

"And only I know when it will explode.
You'll never find it! You couldn't even find My Self,
behind you, the strangler twin who wants you to die,
needs your pretty pastel corpse in a shroud of snow!"
Interesting that the others, at last alert to danger,
shove open the windows of the sleek Express

without hesitation. Survival, not self-express-
ion, makes them dash, makes them explode
like cannonballs through the windows, each fragile self
toughly trusting its instinct not to die,
though the train, at top speed, roostertails through snow.
Its sleety lurching stings my cheeks with danger.

My tears turn to frost! Alone with My Self, my danger
is extreme. No word, no gesture can express
such fear. I freeze, a deer ambushed in snow.
At any instant the hidden bomb will explode.
Or not. My numb mind weighs its fears: to die,
or live in wretched terror of My Self?

I no longer know who I am. How, then, can self-
preservation act to fling me out of danger,
through the window, down the snowbank? There to die,
perhaps, on traitor rocks as the Express
grows tiny, then vast, a supernova exploding,
raining exquisite debris on the torn snow?

But no. It must be midnight. In a mantle of snow
with hoarfrost guard hairs, I come to my queenly self,
clutching a crystal bud vase. Whatever exploded
has left me tranquil. I'm chilled, but far from danger.
From help as well. Those strangers on the Express
now face the same predicament. They'll die

in a waste of black snow, dim stars. As I must die,
as well. But what are these boot tracks in the snow,
that vulpine barking trying to express

its outrage at the risk to all the selves,
dispersed and isolate, in deadly danger?
It is—oh, horror!—My Self, ready to explode.

"Didn't any of you gentlefolk notice an explosion?
Do you plan to wait like huddled sheep to die?
Are your brains too dim with cold to see the dangers
of hunger, thirst, no shelter from the snow?
We've got to organize, to rouse ourselves,
we orphans of the *Orient Express!*

"Still can't get moving? Then try to imagine—Italy!
You're at a café; the taste of *espresso* explodes
on your famished tastebuds. How fine it feels to be selfish!
When that voluptuous flavor finally dies,
there are dozens as fine: *gelati* like sensuous snow
frosting exotic fruits, *biscotti* drenched dangerously

"in chocolate or liqueurs . . . But wait, you fools, the danger
is real, here, *now!* To see you dreaming of Italy
in hypothermic torpor makes me explode!
You over there! Communing with yourself
won't bring us food or firewood. Work or die,
that's how we stay alive! Look up, it's starting to snow

"again! It's almost dark. And when fresh snow
and wind conspire to blind us, we're all in danger,
in mortal danger. Forget about Italy,
the distant mountains, the flowers, the sun exploding
its rays on the spangled sea. If you can't forget yourselves
and work together now, you're going to die!"

My Self's raging eloquence stirred us all. The die
was cast, her way, of course. From out of the snowy
shadows drifted other passengers. The collective danger
in My Self's coercion scared us. But hopes of Italy
made us form work groups and scatter, a stealthy explosion
of warm-blooded wraiths through the forest. Each struggling self

cherished itself again. But fear of My Self
drove us hard. There are so many ways to die.
We had hidden, hung back, hesitated. To sleep in snow,
to wake to hunger and frostbite, seemed gentler dangers
—for how many really believed we could make it to Italy?—
than the ravening will of My Self, who could explode

in a violent instant, who doubtless still carried explosives,
firearms, daggers, and poisons concealed on herself.
Yet we did survive. Brute will won't let you die.
We built fires, then lean-tos, then igloos hacked from snow.
We foraged, hoarded supplies. There were few real dangers.
But finally My Self demanded a palace! *In the Italian*

manner! Then, by twos and threes, hungry for Italy
all the others sneaked off through the snow, leaving me to My Self.
Who, now, is more dangerous? Which will explode? Who must die?

FIRE SHADOWS

In memoriam William Sheridan Pittman and Richard Ronan

i.

I open the door.
You are there
in your outsize, empty sweatsuit, bodiless,
face radiant with greeting.
Acrobat flung between worlds,
you swing toward me on a slant trapeze of sunlight.

Fire shadow, hungry ghost—
a hundred, a thousand times
I open the door.
You are there.

ii.

Nineteen, from a bounty of hundreds,
found in a plastic bag, after five years of drying,
ribbed, shriveled, desiccated, wrecked, alliterative
umbrella, printed with mummified clots of roses.
Better to see them as some derelict gadget,
light as a tacky postcard, scratch and sniff,
suffused with nostalgic, faintly urinous sweetness.

It does nobody any good, this dry, spent cherishing.

iii. *Cha-jin*

These are its beauties—

thin wheel-ridged ocher shape fitted to palm,
a lopsided, intimate wash of black slip, rim to mouth,

ripe fire blush on both sides, visceral fevers
slaked in stone, harsh, *zangurishita,*

and the willed sea dense and belling in its hollow,
shorebird nail-chitin scraping its gritty flanks.

And these, thrown with wise haste, are its flaws—

wheel blots and spin gouts,
sharp bisque-fired nicks overglazed,
one careless, flying black thumbprint—

and that its master is lost, now, to all ceremony,
the grit of his blazing foamed and steeped in shallows
his fire-marked emblem hollow between my palms.

iv.

Richard said, "Years ago, my sister
saw some neighborhood boys set a live cat on fire.
It ran toward her still blazing,
its back, legs, tail seared black.
It fell into her life like a meteor.

"She put out the flames, drove the boys
away, took the cat to a vet,
then home with her. For five years, it was her pet,
in endless pain, requiring endless treatment.
Yet it seemed entirely ignorant
of what had happened to change its life so terribly.
Incredibly, it had no fear of flames,
but would settle itself as comfortably
by the fire as any ordinary house cat.

"It must never have seen
the fire consuming it.
Bill was like that.

Things I saw—the horror of seeing the doctor, over and over
drive that spike, with a mallet, into his hipbone—
have seared my memory forever.
                                    But he
was heavily drugged, and didn't remember, after.
Even at the last, on the respirator,
going down with *pneumocystis* for the third
time, he never believed that he would die."

v.

Ikebana is ruthless. Its implements
are martial, even sadistic:
snips, wires, spiked kenzans,
and a gadget like a staple puller:
a pair of hinged jaws with razor-sharp inner edges.

So Richard, on my birthday,
grappled with hundreds of blood-
red roses, locking his left hand
on the throat of each in turn,
while the right, with a single expert
ripping slide, stripped skin,
thorns, foliage from stems
longer than my legs.
                                    Barbed wire
piled up on the kitchen counter, yards of raveling
stem-peel spiked with thorns.
Each flayed American Beauty wore a saw-toothed
dog collar of four glossy compound leaves.

Next, the master's eye for literal scorched earth
fixed on a stoneware barrel that once held rice.
Stem on denuded stem, he built a wide,
then tightening spiral.
The pot became a blood-drenched
hearth, the roses sacrificial hearts
hurled throbbing on the pyre.

Richard was gray and trembling
with fatigue that day; had risen
at four to be first at the flower market. The fire
he built for me revived him.
And I, for the longest while, was taken in—
the extravagance, the Hollywood glamour of the gesture—

It has taken years to comprehend
how, dying, he laid that fire to shadow memory,
a ghat left burning
where my life flows toward the sea.

vi.

The master potter Fujiwara speaks:

I was forty when I first felt clay.
Dug from below Imbe
rice fields in winter, picked over, sieved,
foot-kneaded, drained, then ripened
for three years, the clay of Bizen
is superb. To touch it
is to become, as I did, completely dedicated.
Between hands and wheel, forms spring up, elastic, animated—
as many, though I am old, as birds of the air!

I fire once a year, in November.
The weather is perfect. Still, planning
how to load the kiln makes my head ache.
Unglazed, the color and texture
of each pot depends on order, placement, chance.
Fire follows the easiest route, its path marked as shadow.
I stack thin tokkuri *next to brawny* tsubo,
bind bowls with rice straw, scatter
sake cups like butterflies over plates.
Three days to heat the stepped kiln, nine to fire.
Burnt straw, red pine rain down
as ash. A week to cool,

and still half break in firing.
Flickering shadows fixed in dissolution,
their ruined shapes adorn the one in ten
I spare.
     It was to make fire shadows
I laid down my writer's brush and took up clay.